Kundalini Yoga

Learn how to heal your Body naturally by awakening your Kundalini

By Tashi Lingpa

Kundalini Yoga

Copyright 2015 by Tashi Lingpa

All rights reserved in all media. No part of this book may be used or reproduced without written permission, except in the case of brief quotations embodied in critical articles and reviews.

The moral right of Tashi Lingpa as the author of this work has been asserted by her in accordance with the Copyrights, Designs and Patents Act of 1988.

Published in the United States by Awesome Life Resources. 2015

Ebook ASIN: B00LYRE52M

Paperback: 978-1507785539

Table of Contents

Disclaimer

Introduction

An Introduction to Kundalini Yoga

    What is Yoga?

    What is the meaning of Kundalini?

    Origin of Kundalini Yoga

    Science behind Kundalini Yoga

    Frequently Asked Questions about Kundalini Yoga

Benefits of Kundalini Yoga

    Kundalini Yoga - Health benefits

    The Importance of Posture and Breath control

    Understanding the connection between Kundalini and Chakras

Physical and Spiritual Healing through Kundalini Yoga

    Pranayama - Breath Control

    Asanas – The Postures

    Naad - Essence of Sound

    Mudras - Hand gestures

    Dhrist - Eye Awareness

    Bandha: Locking Energy

    Clothing and Time Frame - Points to Remember

Bonus Chapter

Sadhana - Practicing Kundalini Yoga At Home

Conclusion

Thank You!

Preview of "Reiki for Beginners: Learn how to Heal your Body through the Power of Reiki"

What is Reiki?

How does Reiki Work?

Benefits of Reiki

Disclaimer

This Book, 'Kundalini Yoga: Learn how to Heal your Body Naturally by awakening your Kundalini' has been written with an intention of providing you with basic information about awakening your Kundalini and its benefits. The information provided in this Book is meant to be taken as a broad guideline to understanding Kundalini Yoga. Although the author has taken utmost care to make sure that the information provided herein is true and accurate, the readers are advised to take precautions before following any of the instructions and information provided in the book.

The author cannot be held responsible for personal or commercial damage caused because of misinterpreting the contents of this book. The author does not hold responsibility for any loss, damage, or liabilities incurred directly or indirectly with the information contained in this book.

Introduction

In this hectic and fast-paced technology driven world, it is become necessary for everyone to seek and passionately pursue any activity that gives them the most-treasured peace of mind and relaxation. Moving from this mechanical life and into a relaxed and stress-free world is, perhaps, on everyone's mind. From the minute we wake up to the minute we fall dead-tired on the bed, we are running and running faster, just to stay where we are. At times when our old TV and sports are not giving us the kind of mental and spiritual relaxation we are looking for, we are forced to turn to holistic and traditional relaxation techniques.

Traditional, meaningful and holistic healing and relaxation techniques are fast catching up with the moving masses. Although we had started looking at alternative medicine and healing techniques with a lot skepticism, it must be said that we, as a people, have progressed a lot in accepting a number of traditional and oriental healing techniques for physical and spiritual healing. Most of these traditional methods have been around for more than a hundred years, but science and scientific community is just not crediting these techniques for their usefulness.

Yoga, Chakra balancing, Reiki and crystal healing are all gaining popularity throughout the western world, thanks to their immense healing powers. These methods do not use medicines, and do not come with harmful side effects. The person who is using any of these techniques is required to simply understand the method, accept it, follow its rule, and practice it passionately.

One such holistic healing technique is the Kundalini Yoga that cleanses the body and mind. Although Kundalini Yoga is one of the oldest forms of yoga, practiced in ancient India since 500 B.C., it was not until Yogi Bhajan brought it to the West in the 1960's that it became popular. Kundalini Yoga provides a number of health benefits –physical, mental and spiritual wellbeing – to those who practice it regularly. While there are a few controversies that abound performing Kundalini Yoga, it's very many advantages easily override the myths.

An Introduction to Kundalini Yoga

What is Yoga?

Regardless of where we belong to, or what work we do, most of us are used to looking for happiness and fulfillment outside of ourselves. We expect our fancy car and our humongous houses to give us happiness and a sense of satisfaction. Cars, houses, clothes and shoes do provide fulfillment, they manage to lift up our sense of pride and boost our confidence levels and skyrocket our image in the society; however, these feelings of happiness and fulfillment are temporary. None of these things can provide permanent and never-changing happiness. Granted that our car helps us enjoy ourselves, but this car is great only until you get another bigger, better and fancier car. This is the human mind – to always accept change. There is nothing wrong in accepting – and even ferociously seeking – change and happiness. However, we should remember to seek things that will give us ever-lasting happiness, something that doesn't change with the changing times.

We are all living in a make-believe world that has trained us to believe that the outside world gives us everything we want. However, time and time again we have come to realize that this is not true. Our experiences have shown us that the outside world can provide momentary happiness, but cannot completely fulfill our needs and longing for something more meaningful. We have all, at one time or the other, found ourselves longing for the 'real' happiness, and marched towards it just to realize that it lay a little beyond our reach. Even while praying, we are all aware of going through the 'motions' of prayer – folding our hands and closing our eyes – and not 'being' in the moment. We are performing an 'act' rather than being 'aware' of the presence of God. With our thoughts, feelings, and actions perpetually dancing in our minds, it is very difficult to create a calm and peaceful state of mind. However, this state of quietude where the mind and the body are in a state of Oneness can only provide Absolute Bliss and peace of mind. Although it is difficult to achieve this state, it is not impossible.

Normally, every human being spends his energy in understanding the outside world. We make use of our five senses – the sense of touch, smell, vision, taste and sound – to understand and comprehend everything in this world. However, these five senses are not enough to help us understand more complex aspects of life. Depending solely on the five senses, sometimes, gives us false and unreliable information. That is why we find the need to dig deeper into ourselves in order to seek answers to the mind-boggling enigmas of live.

Yoga offers practical step by step methods that do not ask you to disregard your intelligence and emotions or to accept doctrines on blind faith. In fact, yoga requires you to apply your mind in understanding its techniques and to accept its teachings.

Yoga is the science through which the human soul (or mind) consciously communicates with the Supreme Being (or God). The word 'Yoga' is derived from a Sanskrit word called 'Yug' which means 'union'. Thus, by doing yoga, a person is said to join with the Higher Being. Spiritually speaking, yoga helps a person realize the identity of the Paramatma (Supreme Soul). A person's mental modifications are removed when he is performing yoga as it helps him disengage himself from the materialistic worldly pleasures and connect with happiness and peace.

Though a large number of people are under the wrong understanding that yoga is only about physical exercises and breathing techniques have grossly mistaken the true power of performing yoga. Although these 'asanas' have gained immense popularity in the recent years, they are only the most outer parts of a profoundly great science of self-awakening. Not everyone is competent to perform yoga; it is not enough to have pure thoughts and perform good deeds, but knowledge, attention, detachment, dispassion, pure-intellectual functioning and reasoning, meditation and more are required.

Although there are a number of paths, each of these paths led towards the same goal. These specialized branches of Yoga concentrate on one aspect of self-realization.

Hatha Yoga: Hatha means willful and Hatha Yoga involves asanas or postures intended to purify the body, provide better control over internal organs and physical state, and to provide the necessary physical stamina and strength to endure long and rigorous hours of meditation.

Mantra Yoga: Mantra means chant or repetition. Mantra Yoga is the repetition of words – japa – and sacred texts in order to center the consciousness within the body.

Karma Yoga: Karma actually means 'action.' Karma Yoga is performing selfless service to others without concerning yourself with the benefits and results of your actions.

Gyana (Jnana) Yoga: Gyana or Jnana means wisdom. Gyana Yoga means using your intelligence to understand and attain spiritual liberation.

Bhakthi Yoga: Bhakti means devotion. Bhakthi Yoga means feeling all-surrendering devotion to every creature in this universe so that you maintain a devotion that never ends.

Raja Yoga: Raja means royal. Raja Yoga is considered to be the highest path of yoga. According to the Hindu sacred text, Bhagavad Gita, Lord Krishna is supposed to have immortalized this yoga in his conversation with Arjuna. This yoga was formally systemized by a great Indian sage in the second century B.C., Patanjali. This yoga combines the essence of all the various paths.

There are eight important aspects (eight fold path) of yoga. They are yama (moral conduct and ahimsa), Niyama (religious observance and self-discipline), Asana (bodily postures), Pranayama (breath control), pratyahara (withdrawal of physical senses), Dharana (concentration), Dyana (meditation) and samadhi (enlightenment and experience of union with the Supreme Consciousness).

Among these eight paths, the first seven help in achieving the final Samadhi.

What is the meaning of Kundalini?

Kundalini is known as the power center in the body. It is in the form of a coiled serpent that resides in the first of the seven chakras – the muladhara chakra. The other chakras in the body are the Svadhisthana chakra, the Manipura chakra, the Anahata chakra, the Vissudha chakra, the Ajna chakra, and the Sahasrara chakra.

The Kundalini is a source of untapped energy residing in the base of the spine – the muladhara chakra – that can be drawn up towards the head – the place of the sahasrara chakra – by practicing yoga. While awakening the power of the Kundalini and drawing her up to the head, you awaken each of the six chakras. You attain liberation, enlightenment or Moksha when this energy reaches the zenith – the crown or the sahasrara chakra.

Kundalini or the coiled serpent resides in the muladhara chakra that is at the base of the body. The muladhara chakra is the seat of Shakthi. The Sahasrara chakra is the highest and most powerful of all the chakras. The Sahasrara chakra is also called as the thousand-petalled lotus that is the seat of Lord Shiva or the Parabrahmam (Supreme Consciousness). The purpose of awakening the Kundalini yoga is to unite the muladhara chakra with the Sahasrara chakra.

In a person who is completely besotted with the worldly pleasures, the power of the coiled serpent or the Kundalini is sleeping. Since we are still enjoying sensual and material pleasures, we are not providing the right stimulus for the Kundalini to awaken. Practicing yoga and following the shastras (or the sacred texts) alone can help awaken the Kundalini in people. The power of yoga can help you awaken your Kundalini or muladhara chakra and not any of the materialistic wealth or worldly influence.

Origin of Kundalini Yoga

Kundalini Yoga is one of the oldest forms of yoga practiced in India. Although yoga, primarily the asanas, has become hugely popular all over the western world, Kundalini Yoga remained fairly secretive and mostly misunderstood. Since it was not taught by many teachers, most of the information about this form of yoga was shrouded in mystery for ages. It was not until Yogi Bhajan popularized Kundalini Yoga in the 1960's that the western world came to know about this powerful yoga technique. However, Kundalini yoga had always been popular in India, where it originated.

The earliest known mention of the Kundalini Yoga can be found in the Yoga – Kundalini Upanishad which is one of the 108 Muthika Upanishads. Kundalini Yoga is also sometimes called as the Laya Yoga which is influenced by Hinduism's shakta and tantra schools. Kundalin (adjective), in Sanskrit means 'circular.' Kundalin (noun) means a 'snake' or a 'coiled snake'. The Kundalini concept belongs to Hatha yoga aspect of yoga. Patanjali's yoga sutras (knowledge of yoga) are known as the main masterpiece of yoga. Although Patanjali is credited with organizing the practices and purpose of various form of yoga, he is not seen as the one who originated the text. He had systemized the content in a proper manner; and the manner in which the content has been presented shows that Patanjali has assumed that the person reading it has the guidance of a teacher. So, it is advisable to perform the

Kundalini yoga with the help of a teacher. Patanjali's yoga sutras were called as the 'classical yoga' since they were intended for the monastic's who had a fairly good idea about yoga and meditation. However, the Kundalini yoga being taught these days is intended for the householders.

In the early 1900's, an Oxford graduate, John Woodroffe, translated a few original Sanskrit texts. He published his most popular book, 'The Serpent Power: The Secrets of Tantric and Shaktic Yoga.' This book became one of the first major sources of information about Indian philosophy and spirituality to the western world. However, Kundalini Yoga was brought to the western world by Yogi Bhajan who brought the previously restricted form of yoga into the mainstream in the 60's. He started the 3HO – the Healthy, Happy and Holy Organization.

Science behind Kundalini Yoga

Since Kundalini Yoga has only recently entered the realm of western society, scientific studies to understand and substantiate its usefulness remain few and far between. However, it is gratifying to note that the scientific community is finally getting interested in looking at this ancient tradition with new eyes. There is no concrete information or scientific proof that the Kundalini yoga has been able to provide insights into the human anatomy. Although most of the physical experiences associated with awakening the Kundalini are still to be substantiated with science, the fact that most of the experiences of Kundalini are subjective and personal should not be undermined.

It is proven beyond a shadow of doubt that the various asanas (postures) pranayama (breath control), mudras (gestures) are useful in maintaining the health of the individual performing the yoga. Regardless of the scientific proof, it is confirmed that the amount of exercise, breath control a person receives is immensely beneficial to their overall physical health. Moreover, meditation is also very helpful in calming the nerves and easing out the stress.

Frequently Asked Questions about Kundalini Yoga

- **Should I become a vegetarian to perform the Kundalini Yoga?**

It is not necessary that you should be or become a vegetarian to perform Kundalini yoga. However, it is advisable that you refrain from eating meat because meat takes a lot of time to get digested. Vegetarian diet digests faster. Meat produces most amount of acid in the stomach; it is the greatest source of harmful cholesterol. Since these days animals are being raised in farms, they are subjected to the harmful effects of steroids, hormones and chemicals that are designed to increase their growth. This is harmful for human beings who consume them. Finally, there are moral reasons for becoming a vegetarian.

- **Can I be a Christian and still perform the Kundalini Yoga?**
  The concept of God in Christianity is entirely different from the concept of God in Hinduism and Kundalini Yoga. However, not every session in Kundalini yoga deal with God or religion. There are a number of kriyas in Kundalini yoga that are purely physical exercises or breathing exercises. The choice to do the mantra (chanting) is purely up to the person.

- **Is it true that I should not eat at least 2 to 3 hours before Kundalini Yoga session?**

It is recommended that you refrain from eating anything at least 2 to 3 hours before starting Kundalini yoga session. The reason being, certain asanas are challenging and require physical workout. With a stomach fully loaded, you are going to find it difficult to stretch and move. A few asanas require you to stand on your head and bend over backwards completely. During these asanas, the food in your stomach will make you feel very uneasy and uncomfortable. Make sure you have digested the food properly before starting any yoga session. That is the reason why the best time to perform Kundalini yoga is early morning as you are unlikely to have your stomach full.

- **How many hours each day should I perform Kundalini Yoga before I can sense any change in me?**
  This is a tough question as there are no hard and fast rules to Kundalini awakening. Each and every person is different, and the path to Kundalini awakening is a purely personal one. Your passion, dedication and concentration are important for Kundalini awakening; however, you should experience and enjoy each and every session and kriya to be able to awaken your coiled serpent.

Benefits of Kundalini Yoga

Kundalini Yoga - Health benefits

There are a number of physical, mental and spiritual benefits of awakening the Kundalini. Apart from improving your physical health, thanks to the number of asanas you are going to perform, this form of yoga helps you stay younger – in mind and in the body.

Kundalini Yoga helps you calm down your mind and relax your body. By helping you relax, Kundalini yoga also helps you make the right decisions, recognize the real and seek permanent happiness. You will be able to steer clear off the confusion and take the right decisions at the right time.

With the amount of physical exercises, and breath control techniques you are going to receive, your immune system, body posture and stamina are going to increase manifold. You will feel and appear more relaxed than ever. You will have more strength and stamina that will help you endure long hours of physical and mental stress. In fact, awakening the Kundalini will also strengthen your spinal cord, nervous system and all your vital organs.

Kundalini yoga, similar to any other form of yoga, relaxes your mind, and lets you enjoy a state of calm and quietude. It can help you clear all your doubts and cravings about the materialist world. Your conscious mind will clear out all the negative images of past lives. You will be able to remember and recognize all your past lives. The lessons learnt in your past lives are etched somewhere in your subconscious mind. Awakening the Kundalini will help you remember old lessons so that you don't have to repeat them all over again. Even if you don't believe in past life and rebirth, you can be sure that the Kundalini has the power to relax your mind completely.

Kundalini yoga involves a certain amount of meditation, in addition to the asanas. You will improve your breathing; build stronger and healthier lungs and heart. A few minutes of Kundalini yoga will keep your energy levels up consistently over the whole day. Since Kundalini Yoga consists of yoga postures, deep breathing techniques, hand gestures, chanting, body locks, and meditation, you can be sure that all your body parts are getting their share of energy boost. Moreover, with meditation, your mental and spiritual health is also taken care of.

The Importance of Posture and Breath control

Kundalini Yoga not only focuses on the postures (or asanas) and breath control (or pranayama); it also lays a lot of importance on chanting, hand gestures (or mudras) and meditation. Like almost all the yoga types, even Kundalini Yoga poses are supposed to be performed in an order to be most effective and less difficult for you to perform. In fact, your flexibility or your weight is less important factors when you are undertaking the Kundalini yoga sessions.

Perfecting a few of the asanas is very important as your ability to stay still in these asanas will have a huge impact on your ability to concentrate on meditation. These asanas and pranayama techniques are designed to help you meditate better. The steadier you are while doing these asanas, the steadier you will be while meditating. You will be able to maintain one-mindedness and concentration for longer periods of time.

Although it is not easy to perfect any of the asanas easily, you should be able to maintain the posture for half an hour every day, so that after a year or so, you will eventually graduate to 3 hours per day. There are close to 84 asanas, but 32 among these are very useful. A few asanas are to be performed while standing, a few while sitting and a few with your legs facing upwards. Among these 84 asanas, four asanas are specifically prescribed for meditation purposes – they are Padmasana, Svasthikasana, Siddhasana, and Sukhasana.

Pranayama or breath control is very important aspect of Kundalini Yoga. 'Prana' is then manifestation of energy that is present in the whole universe. Ordinarily, breath is considered to be the vital force of prana. To be able to control the energy from inside your body, you should first be able to control the vital force of breath. Since you cannot work without your mind, and you mind cannot work without your prana. By controlling your prana, you indirectly control your mind.

According to Hindu philosophy, prana is the life energy that is present in everything in this universe - the same energy that governs everything. If you are able to control your breath, and direct it with your thoughts and willpower will provide great benefits to you. Hatha Yoga firmly believes that the ability to control and subject your breath to your will is more powerful than controlling your mind. The reason being prana or breath is present even when the mind is absent or resting – during your sleep. Prana is seen to play a very important role in Kundalini yoga. If you are able to control and subject the life-force of prana to your will, then you will have the ability to understand and make the universal prana known to you. When you have understood the vital energy that is governing the universe, then you will have nothing to fear about; you know the energy behind all manifestations of the universe.

Similar to how you can control the machine just by controlling the engine, you can control your body and all its vital organs just by controlling the breath. That is one of the main reasons why pranayama is used to gain control over the breath. During meditation, when you bring your mind under your control, your breathing becomes slower and restrained. So, your prana comes under your control. By controlling the prana, you can control all the various vital organs and functions of the body effectively.

Understanding the connection between Kundalini and Chakras

Every one of us has an aura – a glow of light around us – whether we are able to see it or not. Some of us might have a broader and more vibrant aura and some of us might have a pale and think aura. Regardless of how your aura appears, it is real and present. The aura is made up of subtle substance – subtler than your physical body – but real just the same. The aura of a person depends on the person's thoughts, their way of talking, their environment and their emotional state and more. Although most of us cannot see auras, there are people like skilled psychics, yogis and clairvoyants who have the capability and the power to see other people's auras. They also have the power to judge the nature and character of the person just by looking at their aura. We have all, at some time or the other felt an instant connection with people we barely know. Similarly, we have also disliked or felt uncomfortable with certain people. The reason for this is your aura and their aura has some connection. People who are in love will often find their aura and their aura have brushed against each other; and a field of light has formed that surrounds both the partners. Auras are fields of energy that are emanated by the body and they change according to your mood, physical health, mental health, emotions and state of being.

Chakras are the energy centers present inside the body and are fixed in their place. There are seven chakras in our body and each of these chakras has a purpose, a location, a color and relate to a certain aspect of life. The seven chakras are the Muladhara, svadhishthana, Manipuri, anahata, vissuddha, ajna, sahasrara chakra. Each and every chakra has a specific location in the body. Although your aura's color changes with your changing mood, changing the appearance of your chakra needs much more than just a change in mood. A strong and life changing event has the power to change the appearance of your chakras.

The root chakra or the muladhara chakra is located at the base of the spine. The muladhara chakra is the abode of Kundalini. This female force of power, when awakened, has the capability to transform your life completely. In fact, the purpose of Kundalini yoga is to awaken the coiled serpent from its slumber. The powerful Kundalini force wakes and rises through the body, from the muladhara (root) chakra to the sahasrara (crown) chakra; it travels and raises each and every chakra in its wake. By awakening each of the seven chakras, you will be able to develop immense psychic and spiritual abilities. You will receive immense power that can only culminate in attaining higher levels of consciousness, liberation, enlightenment and being a part of the greater cosmic consciousness.

Physical and Spiritual Healing through Kundalini Yoga

Pranayama - Breath Control

So, who taught you how to breathe? No one. No one teaches us how to breathe; it is almost a given that you know how to breathe. Yes, of course, we know how to breathe, but are you doing it correctly. If you notice your breathing structure, you will see that you tend to take in short shallow breaths and into the upper chest without working your stomach. Your breath tends to become shallow and quicker when you are tensed or angry.

By deepening your breath, you have the ability to reduce your blood pressure, change your heart rate and improve your overall health. Prana is the universal principle of energy, that is both static and dynamic, all pervading and exists in all living forms in this universe. Pranavayu is the life force of this universal energy that we inhale and exhale.

Pranayama is one of the techniques used in yoga, especially Kundalini yoga that is helpful in awakening the dormant coiled serpent. There are various pranayama techniques; each technique suits the needs of people with different temperament, constitution and requirements. Some of the pranayama exercises used in Kundalini yoga are:

Sukha Purvaka Pranayama:

1. Sit in padmasana posture.
2. With your right thumb, close your right nostril.
3. Inhale slowly through your left nostril. Count to 10 slowly.
4. Imagine taking in the life energy and filling your lungs with it.
5. Now, close the left nostril with your right hand ring finger and little finger.
6. Retain the breath. Count till 15.
7. Now, remove the right hand thumb from your right nostril and exhale slowly.
8. Repeat the same by inhaling through your left nostril and exhaling through your right nostril.
9. This whole process is one pranayama. If you are a beginner, doing 12 pranayamas per day is advisable. Do 6 in the morning and 6 in the evening.
10. The inhalation, retention and exhalation ratio is 1:4:2. Maintain this regardless of the number of pranayama sets you do in a day.

Bhasktrika:

1. Inhaling and exhaling rapidly is the hallmark of this pranayama.
2. Sit in padmasana or sukhasana posture.
3. Close your mouth. Don't strain.
4. Quickly inhale and exhale at least 20 times in rapid succession.

5. While inhaling and exhaling, dilate and contract your lungs.
6. Forcibly exhale in rapid succession. A hissing sound is produced during this practice.
7. Once you complete 20 inhalations and exhalations, take a deep breath.
8. Retain this for as long as you can and exhale slowly.
9. This completes one Bhastrika exercise.
10. Start doing 3 Bhastrika pranayama in the morning and 3 in the evening.

Points to note while practicing pranayama:

1. Practicing pranayama in the morning is beneficial. Start early morning, after your morning ablutions.
2. Always sit in a comfortable posture. Make sure you do not slouch and do not keep your spine rod stiff as well.
3. The best postures for performing pranayama are the padmasana, sukhasana or the siddhasana.
4. Always practice pranayama in a dry, clean and well-ventilated room.
5. Sit still while doing this; don't keep fidgeting or moving about.
6. Clean your nostrils before you start the breathing exercises.
7. Do not strain your facial muscles while doing these exercises. You need not strain or contort your muscles. In case, you are not able to maintain your breath for long, don't fret. With practice, everyone will become experts.

8. Don't expect immediate results. If you are expecting to see a drastic change in your system after a few minutes of pranayama, you are mistaken. You should be patient, and practice regularly.
9. You might keep count of your inhalation, retention and exhalation in the initial stages of practicing pranayama. However, if it is disturbing you or if you are not willing to concentrate on it, you can avoid it. Your lungs will let you know their threshold.
10. Do not perform pranayama till you are completely exhausted. Pranayama is not supposed to weaken or diminish your energy levels. You have to feel fresh and energetic while performing pranayama.
11. Rest for a while after the exercise. Don't bathe or dry yourself under cold draughts of air.
12. Always start slow. Once you are sure that you can take more, and then slowly increase the count.

Asanas – The Postures

Most of the time, we never notice the way we sit. We assume that we have the perfect posture and a straight spine. However, you will start to how difficult it is to sit in sukhasana – the easy pose – for a considerable amount of time because you have spent so many hours slouching over your desk. One of the biggest challenges of Kundalini yoga is maintaining the posture for long periods of time. You should be able to maintain the perfect asana, without shaking or fidgeting for at least a few hours. Only when you are able to master these asanas – the Padmasana, Svasthikasana, Siddhasana and the Sukhasana – will you be able to master meditation and awaken the Kundalini. Although there are a number of asanas, only a few of them are being used these days. Let us look at some of the most commonly used and beneficial asanas.

1. Padmasana

    a. Sit on the ground with your spine erect
    b. Spread your legs forward.
    c. Slowly, place the right foot on your left thigh
    d. And place your left foot on your right thigh
    e. Place your wrists on the knee joints.
    f. Lock your thumb with your index finger into a finger lock.
    g. Or, let your index finger touch the middle of your thumb.

h. This is the best asana for meditation, and chanting.

2. Svasthikasana

   a. Sit on the floor with your spine erect.
   b. Spread your legs forward
   c. Slowly, fold your left leg and place the left heel near your groin
   d. Now, fold your right leg over the left leg
   e. Your right leg heel should rest in the place made between the thigh and the calf of the left leg.
   f. This is a comfortable asana, which can be used for meditation and japa.

3. Siddhasana

   a. Sit straight with your spine erect.
   b. Place your right leg on your left leg with the right heel near your groin area
   c. Now, slowly place your left leg over your left leg with the heel of your left leg near the groin area.
   d. The legs should be placed very neatly. Both your ankles should touch each other.
   e. You can place your hands on the knee joints
   f. This is a perfect asana for meditation.

4. Sukhasana

Sukhasana is any pose that you are comfortable in. It doesn't mean that you can slouch or bend. You should see to it that your spine is always straight. If people older than 40 are starting to do yoga, they might not be able to get into padmasana or svasthikasana very easily. That is why they are allowed to sit in sukhasana.

5. Vajrasana

   a. Stand keeping your legs close together, feet and knees of both feet touching.
   b. Slowly lower yourself down and sit on your feet.
   c. Your body weight will rest on your knees and feet.
   d. Although you might feel a little pain initially, you will find that this asana is comfortable after a period of time.
   e. Make sure that your spine, neck and head are all in one straight line.

6. Virasana

   a. This is best suited for meditation and chanting.
   b. Stand in a tall kneeling position
   c. Spread your feet apart – with your feet farther away than your knees.
   d. Slowly sit down.
   e. Sit down between your feet. Your buttocks should rest on the floor between your feet comfortably. If you are uncomfortable, then using a thick block to support your buttocks is a good idea.

f. Your spine, head and neck should be erect but not too stiff.

Sarvangasana, sirshasana, matsyasana, ardha matsyendrasana and urdhva padmasana are some of the other popular asanas in Kundalini Yoga.

Naad - Essence of Sound

Naad is the essence of all sounds present in the universe. In addition to mantra chanting, you must also know about 'naad' when looking to awaken the Kundalini. Naad is a vibration – a common frequency – that is present in everything in the universe. It is one common sound or frequency; it is something like a code to universal language of mankind.

Thousands of years ago, the great Indian sages recognized the fact that the whole universe has a common vibration or a frequency. They found out that the universe is not stationary – something that the modern day scientists are only now discovering. Since everything in this world is in constant movement, every single element in this universe is also in a constant state of movement. This vibration is then manifested to us in the form of energy – light and sound. The limited human senses are able to perceive only a fraction of this all-pervading vibration. However, when we wake up our Kundalini and achieve higher consciousness, we are able to tap into the Super-conscious awareness by the use of mantras. By creating a vibration that is proportional to the vibration of the Creative sound or the all-pervading sound, we are able to achieve Oneness with the highest level of Consciousness.

Since everything in this universe is constantly vibrating, chanting specific mantras produces certain types of frequency and vibrations in the body. When you are producing particular type of sounds, you gain the capability to tap into the rich and common source of the universe.

Using mantras to awaken the Kundalini is one of the most important parts of the yoga. Some of the mantras used for Kundalini yoga are composed in Punjabi – an Indian language. Although composed in Punjabi, these mantras are written in ancient Gurmukhi script. While it is true that without understanding the meaning of the mantras, it is very difficult to use it with conviction, you should also remember that each of these mantras produce a particular sound – with the right vowels and consonants, stress and intonations. When you do not use these sounds, the very purpose of the mantra gets negated. However, to help you concentrate better, you can first understand the language or the mantra and then get the diction right before using it.

So, before chanting the mantras, it is important that you understand its various benefits. Your mouth has both hard palate and soft palate. Hard palate is the roof of the mouth, and it has close to 84 meridians points present in it. When you utter words or sounds, your tongue touches these meridian points, and thereby stimulating the secretion of certain chemicals in the brain – such as neurotransmission fluids. So, every time you speak or utter sounds, your tongue starts to stimulate the meridian points, and thereby stimulating its connected glands.

There are three main elements to understanding the science of naad – the rhythm, the projection and the pronunciation. It is crucial that you follow the precise rhythm of the mantra while chanting. You should also remember to maintain the correct number of beats as well. Proper enunciation, intonation and mainly pronunciation are also very important if you want your tongue to put the right amount of pressure on the meridian points.

Mantras are not just a couple of poems for chanting or just some lines to keep your mind busy. Mantras have a specific purpose, a reason and a science behind them. Sound is one form of energy that has the power and the structure to effect a change in the human mind, the chakras and the human psyche.

Some of the popular mantras used in Kundalini Yoga are:

Om is recognized as the sound of the universe. A deep 'Om' sound emanating from the base of your stomach is very useful. This sound is prevalent everywhere – from the thundering sounds of the ocean to the silent monotonous and airy sound coming from a sea shell. The 'Om' sound is truly present everywhere you look. '**Om**' is the stable, inert and unchanging vibration of the universe whereas '**Ong**' is the creative force present in the universe that makes things happen on the Earth. You use this energy and vibration to be able to connect to the higher consciousness creativity so that you are able to perform in the physical dimension.

Ong Namo, Guru Dev Namo – 'Adi Mantra' or the first mantra, this precedes the practice of Kundalini yoga. **Ong** is the manifestation of the higher creative energy. **Namo** means greetings, **Guru** is wisdom or teacher, **Dev** means divine or God, and the last **Namo** reaffirms the reverence we feel for the Supreme consciousness. Overall it means, '*I call upon to the Divine Wisdom.*' You initiate any yoga practice with this mantra- filled with humility and reverence.

Ad Guray Nameh, Jugad Guray Nameh. Sat Guray Nameh, Siri Guru Devay Nameh – This is a powerful mantra chanted for seeking protection. The meaning of this mantra is '*I bow or pay reverence to the primal teacher / wisdom. I pay respects/ or bow to the wisdom of the ages. I bow to the True Knowledge, and I bow to the greater unseen wisdom.*

Ek Ong Kar, Sat Nam, Karta Purakh, Nirbhao, Nirvair, Akaal Murat, Ajuni, Sai Bhang, Gur Prasad, Jap, Aad Such, Jugaad Such, Habhe Such, Nanak Hosi Bhee Such – This is the mula mantra of the Kundalini Yoga. Mula means 'root' or the 'source' mantra. The meaning of this mantra is '*The Creator is One. His Name is Truth. He performs everything. He is Fearless, without hatred or anger, everlasting, timeless, non-temporal or undying, beyond life and death, self-existing, self-realized through the Grace of Guru. Meditate – He was true in the very beginning, He was true throughout the ages, He is true even now, and Guru Nanak will always be true.*'

Mudras - Hand gestures

Your hands are the mirrors to your psyche in many ways; they are not merely functional parts of your body. Your health, consciousness, emotions and behaviors are mapped in your hands. By touching, stretching, crossing and curling your hands, you have the ability to allow energy flow from your body to mind. The position you give your hand is called the mudra, and your fingers can create a number of different mudras as well. Some of the mudras used in Kundalini Yoga are:

Pranam: Palms of both the hands are pressed together with both palms and fingers touching completely. This mudra is very important as it balances the yin and yang of the body. The negative and positive sides of the body are neutralized, and a neutral space in the electromagnetic field is created. The joint of the thumbs should align with the breast bone.

Gyana (Jnana) Mudra: The tip of the right hand thumb should touch the tip of the right hand index finger (fore finger). The same should be done on the left hand side as well. This stimulates ability of the person and knowledge. The fore finger or the index finger is symbolized by the planet Jupiter while the thumb represents the person's ego. When the Gyana Mudra is used during meditation, there is an increase in the sense of peace and calmness. Moreover, you can also do the Gyana mudra by holding down the index finger under the first joint of the thumb.

Shuni Mudra: The tip of the middle finger should touch the tip of the thumb. The middle finger is symbolized by the planet Saturn. This mudra gives patience.

Ravi Mudra: The tip of the ring finger should touch the tip of the thumb. The ring finger is symbolized by the Sun or the planet Uranus. This mudra gives health, strength, intuition and sexuality.

Buddhi Mudra: The tip of the little finger should touch the tip of the thumb. The little finger is symbolized by the planet Mercury. This mudra gives clear, sharp and intuitive communication.

While doing any of these mudras, all the other fingers should always be straight.

Dhrist - Eye Awareness

Yoga exercises for the eyes are also an essential part of Kundalini awakening. Dhrist means vision or seeing. The Science of focus helps improve your vision and concentration just how asanas help your body improve its strength and flexibility. By forcing you to focus on a particular point, yogis and guru help you from getting distracted with the things in front of you. Moreover, when you focus your eyes on any particular object, you tend to increase eye awareness and concentration.

There are a number of eye focus exercises used before meditation, some of the more popular ones are:

Focus your eyes on the Third Eye point or the Brow Chakra: Close your eyes and gently raise it to meet the Brow point or the point a little above your eyebrows. This is where Ajna chakra is located, and when this eye meditation is performed, it stimulates the pituitary glands.

Focus your eyes on the tip of your nose: Cross your eyes slightly in such a way that they point to the tip of the nose. This exercise stimulates the pineal glands and helps control the mind.

Focus your eyes on the tip of your chin: Close your eyes and roll down your eyes to the center of your chin. This location is said to correspond with the moon center. It helps in calming down your mind.

Focus your eyes on the Top of your head or Crown Chakra: Close your eyes, and slowly roll your eyes upwards. It should feel as if you are looking upwards towards the center of your head. This is the place of the Crown chakra or the sahasrara chakra.

These eye yoga exercises help improve your vision, concentration, strengthen your core eye muscles, coordination between your eyes and relax and distress your eyes.

Bandha: Locking Energy

Bandhas or locks are primary aspects of Kundalini Yoga. These locks or contractions of particular muscles in key parts of the body help improve the effectiveness of the Yoga. These locks or bandhas allow free flow of energy throughout the physical body and its seven chakras. Bandhas clear out blocked energy passageways so that there is free energy flow in your body. Moreover, bandhas bring in balance, harmony and peace of mind. Some of the most popular Kundalini yoga bandhas are:

Mula Bandha: This is the root bandha used in Kundalini yoga, even though; it is one of the most difficult locks. This root lock directs sexual energy into constructive creative energy. Root lock consists of three different parts.

- Sit comfortably
- Slowly, contract your anal sphincter muscles.
- Lift these muscles upwards and inwards
- If you are unable to locate the muscles, try locating the muscles you would use when you are trying to stem the flow of urine.
- Keep these muscles contracted
- Contract the sex organs area as well
- Contract your abdominal muscles towards the end of the spine
- All these three actions should be done simultaneously.
- You can breathe in or breathe out during the root lock

Jalandhar Bandha: This is one of the most basic badhas used in Kundalini yoga. Whenever you are not required to move your head, this bandha is applied – during meditation, and pranayama.

- Sit comfortably with your neck and spine in a straight line.
- Slowly, lift up your chest and sternum
- Now is the tricky part. You have to stretch the back of your neck by pulling your chin inwards towards the back of the neck
- You should not tilt your head forward or side ward
- Don't strain your facial muscles. Keep your neck muscles loose.
- Do not put your head down

Uddhiyana Bandha: Uddhiyana bandha or the diaphragm muscles allows for better energy transfer between your heart muscles and lower torso.

- Make sure you are doing this lock under partially empty stomach
- Exhale completely while doing this lock
- Sit in a comfortable position with your spine straight
- Inhale and exhale completely and hold your breath after exhalation
- Pull the area above your navel inwards towards your spine
- Maintain your chest position
- Bring the lower thoracic spine forward

- Maintain this lock for as long as you can bear it. You should not feel any strain while maintaining this lock.
- Release it gradually. Relax your abdomen muscles while slowly inhaling.

Maha Bandha: This is the maha bandha or greatest lock in Kundalini yoga. You should apply all the three locks at the same time while keeping your breath out. It has to be practiced during meditation, and pranayama exercises. You have to first apply the mula bandha – first inhale, exhale, apply the mula bandha and inhale. Then exhale, apply the uddhiyana bandha, and then inhale. Relax and then apply the Jalandhar bandha and relax it. Keep repeating these exercises for at least 3 times continuously. Maintain the same order while performing the maha bandha.

Clothing and Time Frame - Points to Remember

- Make sure you wear comfortable, cotton clothes. These clothes should not be too tight or too loose. Snug fitting, comfortable, cotton clothes are perfect for practicing Kundalini Yoga.
- Kundalini yoga is best practiced bare-foot.
- You can use a Yoga mat for practicing this yoga.
- As long as you are able to sit in the asanas comfortably, you need not use cushions or thick pillows. If you are unable to sit in any of the asanas, you can make use of cushions.
- Use a blanket to cover yourself after you have completed one yoga kriya. Usually, at the end of every asana session, you will be given some time to relax. You will get into the relaxation pose or the shavasana. Since your body's temperature tends to drop down in the shavasana posture, you can use a blanket to cover yourself up.
- Perform every kriya – pranayama, asana or the mudra – only until you are comfortable with it. The minute you realize that you are unable to hold your breath or the pose, you can relax immediately. The purpose of the yoga is to help you relax, rejuvenate and refresh. You should come out of a yoga session feeling tired or in pain.

Bonus Chapter

Sadhana - Practicing Kundalini Yoga At Home

Before sketching out your everyday practice session, you should take into consideration some very important guidelines for Kundalini practice.

- Make sure you wear comfortable, cotton clothes – anything that is snug fit is good.
- Never perform asanas on a full stomach. Certain asanas require extensive body stretching and movement, and the food in your stomach will start reminding you of its presence more often than you might like it.
- If you think, you are likely to get hungry during a yoga session, eat a light non-fatty and non-caffeine food and drink.
- Keep a bottle of water handy.
- You might sweat during certain sessions, but don't sit in a cold draught to dry off. Take a bath if you feel extremely tired but after cooling off your body temperature.
- Keep a blanket handy, you might need it to cover yourself during shavasana.
- Use a sturdy and non-slippery yoga mat
- Remember Kundalini yoga has to be performed barefoot.

KUNDALINI YOGA • 43

- Clean your nostrils before starting pranayama
- Don't get into challenging asanas immediately after starting the yoga session. Always start the session with a few warm ups and relaxation techniques
- Never perform an asana or breathing exercise if you become uncomfortable or if it becomes painful. Stop it, slowly. Use your common sense to avoid injuries.
- Although the count for each pranayama exercise is available, if you are unsure of meeting the count, reduce it to your comfort level. If you can't retain your breath for 15 seconds, then make it 10 and slowly increase it.
- Do not overdo any of the exercises. If you want to see drastic change in yourself within a week or so, it is time you changed your opinion about yoga itself. Make sure you are consistent and patient. Don't be too hard on yourself and don't lose passion too soon.
- Always have a teacher to instruct you. It is better that a teacher or a guru instructs you initially. Once you are sure of yourself, you can start practicing at home by yourself.
- The best time of the day to practice Kundalini yoga is the morning.
- Early morning, between 3 and 4 in the morning, is called as 'Brahma Muhurtam' or 'Divine Time.' This is the perfect time to work on Kundalini awakening.
- Practice the yoga in a clean, well-ventilated and spacious room.
- Never practice Kundalini yoga or any other yoga under the influence of alcohol.

- Check with your medical practioners if you are taking prescription medication. Make sure your medical practioners knows about your yoga sessions.
- If you are pregnant, make sure your yoga teacher knows about it. There are specific yoga asanas and kriyas that are catered to meet the needs of a pre-natal and post-natal woman.

Conclusion

Kundalini Yoga is more of a personal awakening than awakening a mystical coiled serpent lying dormant in you. When you are able to truly awaken this coiled serpent, you understand and appreciate the Greater Consciousness of the Universe. You will truly rise above the normal and mundane aspects of life and become one with the One.

Apart from dedication and passion, you have to enjoy and appreciate each and every aspect of Kundalini yoga completely. Understand the yoga, its nature, its beginning, and the reasons for its existence, its benefits, and its purpose before doing it. Whether you are looking to find God or trying to understand the creation, whether you want know the meaning of True Bliss or trying to answer the biggest unanswered question of human kind 'Who am I? What is my purpose? – Kundalini Yoga has the potential to help you – in this life and beyond.

Thank You!

Thank you for purchasing this book! I hope the book was able to help you understand the benefits of practicing Kundalini Yoga and motivated you enough to learn and practice the techniques of Kundalini Yoga!

Finally, if you enjoyed this book, please take the time to share your thoughts and post a review on Amazon.

This feedback will help me to continue writing the kind of books that would give you the maximum value and results. Thank you once again and good luck!

Preview of "Reiki for Beginners: Learn how to Heal your Body through the Power of Reiki"

What is Reiki?

One of the first experiences a child has, minutes after being born, is the feeling of being touched, of being held and felt. A child's primary worldly experience starts with touch – even before the child can understand taste, smell, hearing and sight. Therefore, touch is one of the primal, basic and most fundamental aspects of growing up. It is a very important part of human development. It is not taught; it is instinctual response – a mother's caring touch to soothe a crying child, a handshake to greet, friend's hi-five, or a pat on the back by your coach! The need to be comforted with a touch is something that has shaped and continues to shape the human kind.

Touch has not remained as an instinctive or as a key bonding element in human development. People, for generations, have been using touch as a means to heal self and others. Human touch has immense potential to comfort, soothe, encourage, motivate, love and heal. One healing technique that uses the power of touch extensively is Reiki. Reiki is a natural healing method that works by channeling the power of energy through your hands.

Reiki is a combination of two Japanese characters; the character 'Rei' means 'Universal' and the character 'Ki' means 'vital life energy.' Although most websites and manuals give this meaning for the word 'Reiki', we should consider the fact that each character of the Japanese has varied levels of meanings. So, it is impossible to translate Japanese into English, without running into certain difficulties. In modern dictionaries that provide meaning to everyday Japanese words, Rei is described as a ghost and RI is described as steam – both terms are far from the meaning we are looking at. These definitions do not serve our purpose; however, if we are to consider reiki as a spiritual healing process, then Rei would mean the guiding force behind creation, universal energy and Higher Intelligence, and RI would mean the non-tangible energy that is present in every living form in this universe.

Rei is the all-knowing, ever-present and all-pervading source of energy. It is a form of wisdom that is present in everything. It guides us, develops us, helps us in need, and it is all-knowing. It is sometimes referred to as God, and is called by a number of names – depending on the culture and religion you are born in. RI is the energy that flows in every living form – animals, plants and humans. It is that energy which is available in high quantities in a person that makes him feel strong, healthy and happy. However, if the same energy is depleted or low, it can make him feel miserable, weak and tired. Ki is the life force of a person, which we receive through the air we breathe, the food we eat, the sunshine and the water we consume.

Reiki is used to cleanse, balance, clean and remove negative and excess energy present in the body. Reiki does not only cleanse the negativity from the body but also cleans the effects of negative and excess energy from your aura, <u>the seven chakras</u> and the environment. Negative energy is not only the absence of positive energy but also the presence of immense energy that blocks a particular area. When energy is less or more, it leads to stress, trauma, emotional abuse and depression. Reiki has the power to clear the built-up excess energy deposits, and remove blockages. By removing excess negativity from your body, Reiki helps in developing positive energy.

Reiki, once mastered, can be used to heal self and others. A person attuned to the universal energy has the capability to channel it and use it to heal. The healer is tuned in to receive and channel higher vibrations, and to use these vibrations and attunements for healing purposes. Once the healer clears the channel for free flow of energy, it is open forever; this flow of energy can be used by the healer for healing self or others for the rest of his life.

A Reiki practitioners taps into this wonderful source of universal energy, and channels it through his hands. He examines a person, understands his energy levels, and blockages. After reading the body, the Reiki practitioner uses his hands, channels the Universal energy to heal the person. The person is not only physically healed, but his mental, emotional and spiritual healing also takes place. The person's aura and chakras also undergo a thorough and gentle cleansing. It brings a number of physical and emotional benefits to the person. The reason why Reiki treatment is effective is, it starts by treating the cause of the problem rather than providing medication to treat the symptoms. Most modern day medicines cater to the symptoms while trying to treat a condition. Reiki is a natural, simple, thorough, gentle, safe and effective healing technique that focuses on treating the cause of problems rather than the symptoms.

How does Reiki Work?

Reiki uses the power of channeled energy to heal patients. Reiki is not only used to heal a patient physically, it is also used to heal the mind, emotions and spirit of the person. Reiki uses channeled energy to flow into the affected parts of the body. It cleanses the negative energy deposits and fills it with positive energy. The vibratory levels of the aura – energy field around the body – are increased so that it is cleansed off negative feelings and thoughts. By cleansing the aura, a reiki master is able to break away the negative field from the body. By breaking the bad energy fields, the reiki master helps in cleaning, mending and treating the person, opening up the energy pathways, and allowing life force to move freely in and out in a healthy manner.

Rei, in a spiritual sense, is the God concept that is present around us. It makes things work, and everything in the universe happens because of Rei. And being the non-physical energy, ki is the life force present in all living forms in this world. It should be noted that Ki is affected by the moods, feelings and thoughts of the person. When you are healthy, it reflects in your ki levels. Similarly, when you are sick and sad, the Ki levels in your body are at their lowest ebb. In addition to the physical functional condition of the organs in a body, the levels of Ki and its ability to flow in and out of the body freely defines the health of the person. The flow of ki is crucial factor contributing to the physical and mental health of a person. If the free flow of this life energy is disturbed or hindered, the tissues and organs are affected adversely. Therefore, it is imperative that the flow of ki is smooth, seamless and free in order to maintain a healthy, happy and productive life.

There is a common confusion among people as to whether the mind and the brain are one and the same. However, Reiki practitioners believe that the mind is much more than just a grey cells and right and left hemisphere. They believe that the mind doesn't dwell only in the brain; it is present throughout the body. Since the central nervous system is connected to each and every organ in the body, mind is believed to exist in every part of the body. Moreover, mind doesn't stop with being present in the physical body. The mind or energy field extends outside the body too; and this subtle energy field surrounds the body and it is called as the aura. It is common knowledge that our thoughts and feelings present in our mind affect our physical health as well. It is no wonder then that hope and positive thoughts help us heal better. That is why negative thoughts occurring in the mind affect the whole body and not just the brain. These negative thoughts travel to every part of the body and the aura. The place where negative energy gets clogged is the places where the flow of life energy – ki – gets blocked. This hindrance to the flow of ki affects the physical organs and tissues present in these places. Therefore, it is important to cleanse yourself off negative thoughts and feelings very quickly in order to keep yourself free from physical illness.

Reiki masters have the ability to identify the areas where ki is blocked. Once they identify the areas, they respond to the restrictions by removing the blockage. The power of Higher Intelligence guides the Reiki masters to help the person eliminate debilitating negative thoughts and feelings from flooding their mind. As soon as the master is able to remove negativity in thoughts, the ki is able to flow more freely throughout the body and aura. Reiki starts to flow throughout the body as it slowly breaks away clogged negative thoughts from the unconscious mind thus making sure that the positive and healthy ki starts to resume its flow. As soon as this happens, all the unhealthy organs of the body receive proper nourishment.

Reiki treatment is a completely non-invasive, medication-independent, holistic healing technique. This is one of the primary reasons why Reiki is becoming more and more popular among the masses. Reiki is not only used to heal your physical and mental makeup, but it can also be used to treat others in the same manner. It makes use of crystals, <u>chakra balancing</u>, relaxation techniques and hand position to treat.

Benefits of Reiki

- Reiki is a natural and safe healing technique
- Reiki doesn't use medicines or costly equipment for treatment
- Reiki can be used to heal self and others
- Reiki heals the body, mind, and the spirit.
- Reiki is very effective in treating stress and depression. It relives excess stress and anxiety by triggering the body's natural healing abilities.
- Reiki helps you deal with emotional trauma by preventing it from draining your emotions completely.
- Reiki treats the causes of problems, and it does not cater to the symptoms alone.
- Reiki helps in improving and maintaining overall health. It can be used to speed up the recovery process from illness and surgery.
- Reiki helps maintain a perfect balance between emotional stability and physical strength.
- Reiki is perfect tool to help you relax, rejuvenate and decrease levels of anxiety and stress.
- Reiki helps you sleep better
- Reiki is an effective pain relief treatment
- Reiki helps the body cleanse itself off toxins and harmful chemicals
- Reiki doesn't use medication or surgeries to treat.
- Reiki reduces some potential side effects of other medications
- Reiki improves body's overall physical strength, vitality and postpones the ageing process.

- Reiki not only helps recover from illness but also helps you increase your body's immune system that prevents you from falling sick.

Read the rest of "Reiki for Beginners" book here: http://www.amazon.com/dp/B00LXSC1MI

Printed in Great Britain
by Amazon